Soul Gravity
Haiku Sequences

Gamal Elgezeery

Langaa Research & Publishing CIG
Mankon, Bamenda

Publisher
Langaa RPCIG
Langaa Research & Publishing Common Initiative Group
P.O. Box 902 Mankon
Bamenda
North West Region
Cameroon
Langaagrp@gmail.com
www.langaa-rpcig.net

Distributed in and outside N. America by African Books Collective
orders@africanbookscollective.com
www.africanbookscollective.com

ISBN-10: 9956-551-28-7

ISBN-13: 978-9956-551-28-6

About the Author

Gamal Muhammad Abdel-Raouf Muhammad (Pen Name: Gamal Elgezeery), born on August 2, 1973, is an Egyptian poet, storywriter, novelist, critic, translator and academic. He is currently **an associate professor of English literature** at Taibah University, KSA. He teaches English literature and language courses at Suez University (Egypt) and Taibah University (Saudi Arabia). He began his career as a writer in 1991 and his career as an academic in 1999. He has an **MA degree** in English poetry from Cairo University (1998: *Shifting Perspectives in Roy Fuller's Collected Poems 1936-1961*), a **Ph.D. degree** in English poetry from Ain Shams University (2002: *Narrative Aspects in Roger McGough's Poetry 1967-1987*), and an **associate professorship** from Taibah University in February 2018. In January 2014, he co-founded a Facebook group devoted to the art and criticism of microflash fiction. In May 2014, he founded Hemartak Alarja Ebook Publishing. In October 2015, he co-founded (with Mahmoud Al-Rajabi, Jordan) Ketabat Jadida Ebook Publishers to replace Hemartak Alarja.

Elgezeery has got many awards on his poetry, short stories, novels, and critical writings in Arabic. He has published many books in both English and Arabic.

Books and Papers in English: *Narrative Aspects of Roger McGough's Poetry 1967-1987: A Study of the Intersection of Poetry with Fiction* (2011); "Cross-Referencing Nature and Culture in Nol Alembong's *Forest Echoes*" (2013); "Memory and Homecoming in Niyi Osundare's *The Eye of the Earth*" (2013); "'Boundaries Are All Lies': The Fluidity of Boundaries in Linda Hogan's *The Book of Medicines*" (2013); *Human Objectification in Carol Ann Duffy's The World's Wife* (2014); *Little Red Riding Hood: From Orality to Carol Ann Duffy* (2014); "Environmental Terrorism in Peter Wuteh

Vakunta's *Green Rape*" (2014); "Fluid Identity of the Daughter in Jackie Kay's *The Adoption Papers*" (2015); (with Dr. Mohammad Sha'aban Deyab" "Diverging Concepts of the other in Islam: A Comparison between the Original Islamic Perception and Contemporary Muslims' Practice" (2015).

He also translated about 20 books from English into Arabic, published by the Egyptian Supreme Council of Culture.

In Arabic he published more than 30 books, as follows:

Short Story Collections: *Image Mosaic* (Fatafeet Alsura: 2001); *Anxious Debuts* (Bedayat Qaleqa: 2004); *Inscriptions on the Nile Page* (Nuqush Ala Safhet Alnahr: 2009); *The Smell of a Funeral* (Raeehat Ma'atam: 2010); *Blocking Channels* (Ghalq Almaaber: 2010); *The Blazing of Green Questions* (Ishteaal AlAselatal-Khadraa: 2011); *The Road to Tahrir Square.* (Altareeq Ilal-Midaan: 2011); *One Photo is Enough* (Sura Waheda Taqfi: 2018); *Don't Let Me Suck Your Blood* (2020).

Flash Fiction/ Very Short Stories: *Laugh, My Son* (2018).

Microflash Fiction/ Narrative Wamdhas: *A Camera and an Eye Look: 635 Microflash Fictional Texts* (Camera wi Nazrat Ein: 2017); *Injured Eyes: Microflash Fictional Sequences* (Oyoun Jareeha: 2018)

Poetry Collections: *Don't Wait Anyone, Mr. Poetry* (La Tantazer Ahadan Ya Sayyed Alqaseed: 2009); *Signature Party* (Hafl Tawqee'e: 2010); *And We Still keep Our Blooming* (Wa Nazallu Alaal-Eshraq: 2010); *The Voices of an Ancient River* (Aswatu Nahren Qadeem: 2010); *The Map of Rain* (Kharetatul-Matar: 2010); *The Books of the River Lady* (Asfaaru-Sayedatul-Nahri: 2011); *The Girl of the Daylight* (Bental-Nahaar: 2011); *The Square of Mirror* (Midan Al-Maraya: 2011); *Looks of my Soul: Haiku Poetry* (Nazaraat Rouhi: 2018); *Roots of Illumination.* (Jouzour Ishraaq: 2018).

Novels: *A First Match: Six Short Novels* (Shawt Awwal: 2018); *A Chat over the Blue Space* (Tharthara Fawq Al-Fadaa

Al-Azraq: 2019); *A Prohibited Apple* (Fakeha Muharrama: 2020); *An Unknown Half* (Nisf Majhoul: 2020); *Exit Road* (Tareeq Al-Khorouj: 2020).

Haibun: *Speech Windmills: Haibun Stories* (Tawaheen Al-Kalaam: 2018).

Literary Criticism: *Dialogue with the Text: The Example of the Beginnings of the Century Group* (Alhewaru Ma'al-Nass: Jamaat Bedayat Al-Qarn Namuzajan: 2002)); *Creativity and Culture in Shukri Ayyad's Writings* (Al-ebdaa Wal-Hadhara enda Shukri Ayyad: 2010); *Reading the Revolution Retrospectively: A Study of Al-Sammah Abdullah's Khadija Poems* (2015); *Time and its Implications in Al-Sammah Abdullah's Poetry* (2015); *The Manifestations of Time in Al-Sammah Abdullah's Praise of the High Female* (2015); *Literature and Revolution: A Study of Naguib Mahfouz's Qushtomor* (2015); *A Critical Introduction to Haiku* (2016).

Table of Contents

Introduction

Haiku, as a poetic form, originated in Japan some centuries ago, but this poetic form travelled the world and has been adopted by many cultures as a form capable of accommodating human experience at large. Although the form was originally rooted in nature, natural seasons, and Buddhism, contemporary poetic experience widens this nature to include almost everything.

Although it is a widespread poetic form, haiku is sometimes misunderstood as a mono-level poem that has a descriptive nature. This is largely due to the fact that it is imbued with Japanese and eastern Asian (religious) philosophy, and the traditional or classic Japanese haiku is at least two-level poem and easily understood within the boundaries of its own culture, a culture which does not render itself easily accessible to non-Japanese cultures. This led many poets to have a misconception of the haiku form, seeing it as a poem that describes an aspect of physical nature, as if it were a fragment of something missing or not available. It should be a whole entity with all the elements that enable it to survive in any reading experience.

When reading and translating Japanese and Western haiku into Arabic, I faced many problems. How to render a haiku poem into another language and maintain its life among a different readership? For example, I read all the poems of Basho but was obliged to be selective when translating these poems into Arabic because the subtexts and underlying implications of many poems cannot give themselves easily to translation. The names of many plants, flowers, and elements of nature have implications in

Japanese culture they do not have in other cultures because they are ready or commonly accepted symbols there. Therefore, the poems containing them or having them as symbols seem opaque, vague, fragmented, or lacking something when read by non-Japanese readers. The poems may even acquire completely different meanings and implications when translated into other cultures. Moreover, the translator may resort to a medio-translatological approach and intentionally mistranslates them so that they can be coherent to the new readership. As a result, I selected for translation the poems that can find a new soil to thrive or survive in when rendered into another language and consequently another culture.

When speaking about the migration of a literary form from a culture to another, the Egyptian critic Shukri Ayyad says that every literary form has some cultural residues or layers that are peculiar to its original culture, and these layers are to be dispensed with in order for it to be able to be transplanted into a different culture. We should stick to the core or essence of the form when adapting it to another culture. The same applies to haiku. I have published an ebook in Arabic on the nature of Haiku poetry. In it, I analyzed many haiku poems belonging to many cultures and tried to reach or theorize the soul of haiku. In my opinion, haiku has two or more levels: an experience really or imaginatively present before the perceiver or the writing persona recalls another experience. This act of recalling is based on some sort of similarity or resemblance between the two experiences, and the haiku poem mixes or fuses these experiences in different ways. Although haiku originated as a poem incorporating an element of physical nature, this "nature" can be broadened to include whatever human experiences.

Despite globalization, globalism, dialogue of cultures, universalism, etc., our contemporary culture is largely fragmented. Contemporary people are daily exposed to a flux of data, information, experiences, news, social media, digital influx, transformations, screen manipulations, etc. This is confusing and disorienting and needs some sort of organization at the level of literary expression.

I began writing haiku a dozen or so of years ago, and my early writings were independent or single haiku poems that stand alone. However, I gradually discovered that these single poems aggravate the fragmentation of our contemporary world and that they need to take a larger form that accommodates the single poems into some sort of unity that reflects what I believe to be the unity of the elements of the whole universe and counters our contemporary fragmented experiences. Hence come the sequences included in this collection of haiku.

As severing literature from the real world is a luxury that the former colonized cannot afford, according to Edward Said, we cannot write haiku for aesthetic, or art-for-art's-sake, purposes only, as we have to write art for life's sake. As a poetic form, haiku should be used to express the problems, causes, aspirations, hopes, worries, confusions, and pains of contemporary people(s). Therefore, the haiku sequences in this volume approach and grapple with a wide variety of experiences: individual, collective, social, political, mystic, psychological, natural, psychic, domestic, universal, etc. Each sequence can be read chronologically and spatially: it contains haikus that gradually present successive phases of its poetic experience, and at the same time these phases complete one another and can be regarded as different angles of the same shot. Moreover, all the sequences can be seen as composing a larger sequence that unites and unifies them.

This volume of haiku sequences is an experimentation with the form of haiku. I have read many haiku sequences in English and derived the same conclusion related to individual haiku poems: most of them are esoteric and veiled to the common reader; they require particular readers and are generally written in isolation from general human cares, preoccupations, and interests. We, humans, are an integral part of the universe, and we need to see all the parts interacting with, and complementing, one another. We need to touch the unity that makes all the parts hang together. However, as human beings, we necessarily see everything from our human perspective in a relatively anthropomorphic form, and this perspective differs from a person to another. There is no pure haiku, although many haiku writers claim so. Hypothetically, if an animal or a plant writes a haiku poem, it will write it from its own zoological or botanical perspective/ vantage point and in a manner that will make this perspective accessible to other creatures. Likewise, human haiku should render itself accessible to all humans, and when it celebrates particular aspects of its writer's culture, these aspects should be textually available to public or universal readership. In other words, the emerging democratization of human life and the decolonization of minds, peoples, and even literary forms necessitate dethroning literary elitism and opening literary forms to wide spectrums of literary readership. This collection of sequences tries to publicize haiku as a poetic form capable of living everywhere and accommodating different types and communities of readers.

A Garden of Apples

1
Shyly,
My heart exudes apples;
I look skyward.

2
Stepping
Upon the mountain in awe
Fills my heart with light.

3
My heart is clay.
I frolic in the garden
Without a name.
4
This breeze tells tales.
Who telepathizes with me now &
Teaches me the names?
5
Without a river,
I row my boat
And catch a cloud.

6
As if I were alive,
I swim in clouds
And praise Allah.

7
My national flag
Floats among the clouds
And waves at me.

8
National snipers
Miss their shots at me,
And curse rebels.

9
Within the range
Of national shots,
My eyes blur.

10
We knew each other,
And I do not know me.
Who am I?

11
Adam,
When will fig leaves bud?
I have to know me.

12
Am I an alien?
My memory is bombed &
I still have hope!

2017-2019

Great Peace

1
I am many.
This face is only a drop
In my sea of images.

2
This place
Is faces and mirrors,
And I'm water.

3
I am
In, outside, and from this place.
Am I a barzakh[1]?

4
In this water cup,
I see the river headwater &
The tree that'll grow.

---

[1] In Arabic, barzakh literally means an isthmus. But it has many associations and shades, as it refers to a meeting point or a transitional place or time between two points or things, with a different or opposite thing on each edge of this place or time. For example, the time/place between death and resurrection is called barzakh. In general, the word may apply to everything/ place/ time that transcends the barriers of time and place, although it also means a hidden or unseen barrier or wall.

5

My memory comes back.
It takes shape in birthplace &
Fills my lost colors.

6

This map is erased.
I'll trace its image in my heart
And overtake its eraser.

7

At dawn,
Places and I face towards
The distant river.

8

This scent leads me
To the gates of places and times.
Am I a cocktail?

9

My hand holds yours:
Our hearts are at peace;
This war is helpless.

July 10-19, 2017

A Strange Nightmare

1
No poem
Comes to write me
In a sleepless night.

2
How can I
Exhaust myself to sleep
With my insipid mind?

3
My mind
Cannot create fantasies
In my single bed!

4
In this mazy sleep,
I jump from a scene to another
Without memory?

5
In this foreign land,
I chat with strangers
In an unknown tongue.

6
In transit,
I don't know the next country
I'll travel to.

7
A strange nightmare:
From the sea bottom,
I see my hands white.

8
Among tame sharks
And shades of darkness at sea,
I see myself bleeding.

9
I'll step out
Of this nightmare
To see a lucid scene.

10
I leap
In the dark to catch dreams
For bright memories.

11
In my land,
I sit with my loved ones.
Death looks weirdly!

12
Enough is enough:
Death's eyes smile at me,
And I grimace at him.

13
I would not struggle
With the nightmare if the poem
Came to write me!

14
I fight alone.
My poem and light deserted me
On the battlefield.

15
In this nightmare,
I can rescue myself
And change the scene.

16
On the riverbank,
I dream of the Nile source
While asleep.

17
Water and birds:
I give myself to
A future memory.

18
My commanding voice
Asks me to wake up
And be ascetic.

19
Closing my eyes,
I swim in my present heart
And dismiss my double.
20
An alarm clock:
I turn stupid and switch off
My transmission.

21
At work,
Everything is black and white.
True life is a dream.

March 3, 2018

Gravity Spots

1
A new chapter:
My new line chooses gravity
From another planet.

2
Traffic lights are red,
Drivers choosing to chat
At intersections.

3
A black hole:
This gravity swallows
My body temperature.

4
Cold:
Am I swimming in the sky
Or dead?

5
Migrant birds:
I Lie down on grass
And swim in the sky.

6
After your departure,
Your imagination takes you there
And leaves your body here.

7
In exile,
Borders are monsters tracking
Your memories.

8
From a bright future,
You brighten my mirror
With a fantastic halo.

9
My imagination
Holds a memorial feast
For absent faces.

10
Alone,
I welcome my states and times &
Leave some seats vacant.

11
I'll shake hands
With myself and invite me
To a drink.

12
In my exile,
I meet both my past
And obscure future.

13
Praising Eternal Allah,
I collect the dust of a new life &
Keep faces in my memory

14
Light of my heart,
I yearn for my dust
At your hands.

15
Tunnel light:
I have to finish my work
Before launching.

16
I sneeze:
Will I start a new form of life
And have a miracle?

17
I don't feel sorrow,
Or despair at the spirit of Allah:
Here I am, working.

18
These works are mine.
To whom do those works belong?
Does my road stumble?

19
Notre pater at villages,
Consider me in your amnesia plan;
I am faltering.

20
In the Creator's name,
I contemplate my persistent steps
With a sour smile.

21
I stick
My tongue out at the absurd.
Existence winks at me.

April 4, 2018

Creativity

1
I see
That hidden illumination
In the dark.

2
Insomnia
Occupies the horizon
And me.

3
A challenge:
I smile to the tragedies
My insight discovers.

4
Alone and silent,
My hand communicates
And my head talks.

5
Moonlight:
On a silent desert highway,
Sand has cozy faces.

6
In my car player,
The flash memory is faces, voices,
and extra memory.

7
Fighting gloom,
I meet cheerful company
In my imagination.

8
Unfathomable road:
I enjoy escaping from beasts
In dark forests.

9
It doesn't matter
Whether my eyes see the end
Of the tunnel.

10
My imagination
Creates elaborate images
And tunnel lights.

11
Our hands' touch
On an exhausting road
Empowers us.

12
In the bleak present,
We recall our good memories
To create our future.

February 28, 2018

A Glimmer of Light

1
Give me
An hour of my time
To find my times.

2
While drowning,
I catch my life light
And jump ashore.

3
On the riverbank,
I want to stop
And tickle fish.

4
The whip
Of my livelihood cracks.
I have to go on.

5
On water,
My eye look was flowing
And I was ascending.

6
A riverboat
And fish in my heart:
My memory is deep.

7
Entwined hands
And a voice from the past:
A starburst.

8
My breathless steps
Are existential struggle &
A scanty harvest.

9
A bottleneck:
Who killed me?
Where is my soul?

10
A struggle for food:
A sound of breaking
And soul slums.

11
Clashing voices &
Fighting hands:
Subsistence level.

12
After midnight,
I restore my normal pulse
And ascend to myself.

13
A crash accident:
My soul comes back &
Recognizes my body.

14
Blissful fantasy:
My soul works at full capacity
And asks about me.

15
Silence, shooting:
An executed guillotine &
A rising light.

July 25, 2017

My Support

1
My heart
Is the same and different.
Who is what?

2
My heart
Is teeming with future defeats
My face doesn't tell.

3
Allah,
You're my love and support.
I'm a support too.

4
My wife's tears
Regret a lost life
And hope.

5
My wife is flowers:
We sing of absent life
And thank Allah.

6
You give me.
You deprive me.
I'm grateful.

7
My dead baby
Is a seed of a tree
In heaven.

8
Who rises skyward?
Who will live on a memory
And seek forgiveness?

9
Dawn's call for prayer:
Patience be to me
And praise to you.

10
Allah, relieve my wife
For us to dive into the sea
Of your pleasure.

11
In each step,
We have a trying test.
Are my eyes naked?

12
These life tests
Take me back to school
And bridge a time gap.

13
My wife,
Your sorrow purifies you
And breaks my heart.

14
When sorrows meet,
Hearts expel negative energy
And get company.

15
Say nothing, my wife:
Get off your shoes
And refresh my memory.

November 1, 2017

Addresses

1
I won't ask you
To stay calm.
It is a land of anger.

2
Your calmness there
Is your frustration here.
I'm an expat too.

3
Don't record
My hallucinations now.
Live the moment.

4
After I leave,
Your imagination will summon
Our reunion.

5
This society
Is an edited still picture:
A Photoshop session.

6
Don't expect me
To have an open heart
In a fake milieu.

7
Still water:
Having an open mind is a hell
In this belief jam.
8
I have no idea.
All faces are shape-shifters.
I need a river mirror.

9
Sure, we haven't been here:
These claws suggest we're enemies &
This blood will become water.

10
Close your eyes
And live inside yourself.
It's your fallout shelter.

11
This spaciousness
Is economics' scissors
In human warming.

12
My surviving blood
Feels dead people's claws
In my heart.

13
O sunray,
See you on a night keyboard;
Don't trespass now.

14
Let us play:
Options have left crossroads,
And loads are mountains.

2017

Halal Land

1
Allah,
Don't punish some with others.
This wilderness is many.

2
Beside me,
There're vacant seats in the storm;
You can join.

3
Who burbles?
All cars are departing;
I'll change my tongue.

4
For thirty years,
I've been trying to make sense,
But this year is long.

5
How can I
Create my relief in a land
Of intruders?

6
Don't ask me,
"Who are you?"
I'll know later.

7
When I know
Who I am, we'll paint
Rainbows together.

8
Swirls in view:
But there are no hurricanes
Or echoes!

9
Deadly calm:
Have we argued
With the storm?!

10
Without wings, I fly.
Are roads graveyards,
Or am I slain?

11
I create
This spaciousness elaborately
And curse the morgue.

12
In this morning,
I don't await my people's awards
Or their revival.

13
In this morgue,
You dissect my body,
Without evidence.

14
I wait for
An exhilarating phone call
On this dead network.

15
You see
This thread as bare.
I don't see it so.

16
Shall I
Invoke the storm
To remove your rust?!

17
In each line,
I lend you my eyes.
What is wrong?

18
You don't see yourself.
How can I see you
And myself?

19
Intersecting circles
Without a center:
What is history?

20
At ease,
Centers fight one another.
Where is Halal land?

October 14, 2018 & March 14, 2019

Don't Wait

1
At this dawn,
The light shows in my heart,
Cutting my worries.

2
"An hour ago"
Is an age in this making
Of existence.

3
Turning points:
Is heart-shifting
A melting pot?

4
Tomorrow,
Old mistakes will resurface
And bring us to life.

5
A stalemate:
I must get out of this mire
For a fresh breath.

6
My land
Is hell and heaven, &
All people are equal.

7
My pulse
Escapes hell and heaven
And takes a break.

8
At break,
I ascend to my memory
And make a fortune.

9
I doesn't matter
Whether the light is off or on.
My light is in me.

10
This wailing voice
Says I am real.
I see it cheerful.

11
I dive
Into the my voice and light
In our network.

12
This voice
Is a fresh language
And a pulse.

13
At dinner,
I eat the voice and myself
And glorify Allah.

14
Without a ladder,
Ascend to yourself
And reunite.

15
Don't say clichés.
Hug your light and your heart
With a fresh tongue.

July 26, 2017

A Strange Apple

1
Where
Is my wild imagination
In this bleak milieu?

2
My body
Is lonely
In this empty bed.

3
As such,
You'll drown a trail.
Imagine, my friend.

4
Read
Your earlier imagination
To survive.

5
Like others,
The images of my imagination
Betrayed me.

6
Here I am,
Hallucinating in a room
Full of nightmares.

7
My hallucination
Does not purge me.
Am I dead?

8
Even dying
For her love
Revolts against me.

9
Sweet images
Leave my memory off
In nostalgia.

10
Who has turned off
The light of my imagination
In this loneliness?

11
A minefield:
I haven't turned my cheek
To anyone.

12
Fallout:
My memory is a freak.
It goes its own way.

13
Sorry, my heart.
This apple in your hand
Is strange.

14
My heart,
You cannot recall
The honey river.

15
Bang
Your head against the wall.
You may find your love.

16
Your words alone
May catch your memories.
Go on.

17
Clotted blood:
My heart is full of dead bodies.
Who am I?

March 7, 2018

My Birth Labor

1
These drunk dancers,
Am I among them?
Or is it my name only?

2
A hen,
Surprised by a knife slash,
Sees life as a dance.

3
Whirlpool:
Do I shoot the hollow harvest
Or get lost here?

4
Zikr dance[2]:
Swirling bodies forget everything &
Can't stand the flood.

---

[2] Zikr is an Arabic word which literally means mentioning, remembering, memory, etc. It also refers to the Quran and its recitation. As a practice, it is associated with some sort of religious dance, as in Sufism or Islamic mysticism, where worshippers gather in a mosque or somewhere else and dance back and forth and sometimes in a swirling movement, mentioning Allah and His names and qualities. In this state, they experience euphoria, ecstasy, transports, etc.

5

The river was here.
"His wonder was his tragedy."[3]
I'll be a boat.

6

Mirage:
Have I seen everything
upside down?

7

Headwater:
So why does this river
Kill me?

8

Revelation:
My heart saw a fire
in the valley[4].

9

The river valley
Is full of balloons, nails,
And stagnant ponds.

---

[3] Sabi Moussa. *Seeds of Corruption*. A novel translated from Arabic by Mona Mikhail and published by Interlink Publishing Group, 2002. The original Arabic title is Fasaad Al-Amkina (Corruption of Places). The quote describes Nicolas, the protagonist of the novel who aspires to embrace the soul of pure place or space in the desert of the Red Sea.

[4] An allusion to the fire that that Prophet Moussa (Moses) saw in the holy valley: When he saw a fire and said to his family, "Stay here; indeed, I have perceived a fire; perhaps I can bring you a torch or find at the fire some guidance." (Quran 20 (Taha): 10).

10
A strange mirror:
It reflects life, oxygen
And my skeleton.

11
Let's imagine
Our movements go
With the universe.

12
Don't come closer:
This space around me
Is a shrine.

13
No Entry:
The "Hollow men[5]" are drunk
Around their mirrors!

14
Empty souls:
I won't subscribe to
Calf worshipping.

15
The train passed,
And passengers are pieces
Of worm-eaten wood.

---

[5] The title of a poem by T. S. Eliot.

16
Mojo:
I'll shake the trunk
Of my palm tree.[6]

August 3, 2017

---

[6] An allusion to Mariam (Mary) in the Quran at her labor: "And shake toward you the trunk of the palm tree; it will drop upon you ripe, fresh dates." (Quran: 19 (Mariam Sura): 25).

Step Down, August

1
August, darling,
I can't stand your purgation.
We must separate.

2
I did not die
Or lie to my land:
Why torturing me?

3
This scorching heat
Is souls evaporating out of me.
How can I work?!

4
August, you melt
My fat, bones and soul!
What remains of me?

5
Birth date:
August, I am you child.
Don't forget.

6
August's history:
Old wars resurrecting
Into vengeful spirits.

7
This August
Is a minor Resurrection Day:
Who's the judge?

8
An old river:
Scorching heat burns breath.
What's water?

9
Here I am,
Over but not loving.
Down with August.

10
August and I?
Even nightmares do not have
Such a couple!

11
Volcanoes:
Hands supplicating to the sky &
Vanishing.

12
An image
Of a smiling official on a flagpole.
August is singing.

13
Peace be upon
Departing souls, drying rivers, &
Triers against all odds.

August 11, 2017

Homecoming

1
In my solitude,
I was sewing my days
To get company.

2
Why
Have you provoked me
To leave solitude?

3
Without feet,
You are swaying on the road.
I won't claim arrival.

4
You spoke and stayed.
I don't remember your words
Or see your trail.

5
Without your trail
How can I know you?
This road is mine.

6
In mirage,
You ascend a tree and drop
"Its fruits" to me!

7
My eyes are reborn:
I haven't died,
And you don't live.

8
A flag on my street:
You make passersby believe
That I am you!

9
Brothers?
You ambushed me
On my road, man!

10
Road ambush:
Yes, I'm stuck but see
A bright future.

11
Crossroads:
Leave for the land
Hiring you out.

12
Museum wall:
Your achievements are a made-up
History.

13
I'm in exile.
My father and son
Farm our land.

14
A transit traveler:
My foot was on my land &
The other will be there.

April 7, 2019

Ploughing a Road

1
Nile valley:
My pen ploughs
The sea[7].

2
On the Nile bank,
Upstream and downstream lands
Never meet.

3
A homeland:
What is a nest?
A bird wonders.

4
Withered plants:
I look at my writing happily
And sorrowfully.

5
Ploughing my land,
Snipers are on both sides &
The road is so long.

---

[7] In Arabic, especially Egyptian, culture, to plough the sea means that your attempts and efforts are in vain.

6
Publishing my book,
I am in debt and my publisher
Asks me money!

7
- Pay or perish.
I won't read or publish
Your writings.

8
This is a new road:
It echoes my previous roads
And brand-new ones.

9
- Hey, publisher.
- Respect the dead,
Rebellious writer!

10
Water pen:
My life has fruited, &
Your fossils killed you.

11
Away from fuss,
I catch familiar and new faces
With my heart hook.

12
My land
Has not turned green.
Am I a traveler?

13
This harvest
Is readers passing my timeline
Without notice.

14
No regression.
This land will grow its trees
With my coexistence.

15
Peace be on me
When I embody the future &
Readers revive me.

March 14, 2018

A Song

1
This song
No longer moves me.
Who took its mojo?

2
Stale milieu:
Where are my previous delight
And my heart?

3
Dark visions:
Am I temporarily frozen
Or dead?

4
Outage:
Where is your glimmer
To light my heart?

5
System failure:
Am I scattered
In earning a living?

6
Stalemate:
How can I start
My restore point?

7
No fear.
No calmness;
This maze is nothing.

8
Dead silence:
I can't hear my song.
I can't speak.

9
I am the same
And so is the song.
Where is our chemistry?

March 4, 2018

Fuss

1
Body and soul:
Two opposite directions
And a black whole.

2
Body and soul:
Bleeding maps to the left,
Corpses to the right.

3
Body and soul:
My pulse is there,
And I am here.

4
Body and soul:
On the blank page,
I see white words.

5
Body and soul:
How have I come here
And left myself there?

6
Body and soul:
Won't this poem conclude?
That light is far away.

7
Body and soul:
Let's get to work.
This fuss is deadly.

8
Body and soul:
I'll collect my body scraps
And depart.

March 4, 2018

Too late

1
University dome:
That professor claims piety
And installs a cross for me.

2
You will deny me
After seeing my corrections
Of your draft.

3
It doesn't matter.
I see your mask
Transparent now.

4
You tie
Your mask tight and decry
Opaqueness.

5
I received
Your denial of me.
With indifference.

6
You expect me
To feel pain and stop
Midway!

7
Your bird
Cannot pick my head.
This cross crosses you.

8
How are you, tutor?
You picked the sloping path,
Not the river.

9
How smart you are!
Here you are, an ex-president
Evading my lawsuit.

10
Lord of the stupid,
You suppressed hearts that avoid
Your pollution.

11
Dear sir,
Here you are,
An item on a shelf.

12
Bye for now:
I have chosen
My heart peace.

13
At crossroads,
You are too late for choice.
Enjoy your stalemate.

July 19, 2017

Intersections

1
I kiss Palestine
With a regional novel
And folklore songs.

2
A balcony moon:
Mount Al-Darheeb[8] is awful
And majestic.

3
Al-Aqsa Masjid
Resonates in my memory:
A distant prayer.

4
Closed eyes:
My heart is sight & travel
In this inner light.

5
In the dark,
A light glows on the mountain
And echoes bliss.

---

[8] Mount Al-Darheeb is the spatial protagonist of Sabri Moussa's *Corruption of Places*, published in English as *Seeds of Corruption*..

6
A darkness
Engulfs my heart
In this mountain.

7
My heart ecstasy
Is a communication channel
Through pathways.

8
A fire
Lit on the mountain
Says, "Hey."

9
This lonely fire
Guides my way
And reunites me.

10
Al-Aqsa photo:
My compass flouts
Colonial barriers.

11
Without coordinates,
I flow in all visions
And catch their fish.

July 23, 2017

Nile Symphony

1
Dawn azaan:
My window breeze abroad
Is a village message.

2
An expatriate bird:
My village denying me
Meets me abroad.

3
A breathing morning:
The poem stays up with me.
Who dates us?

4
In exile,
The scent of dawn
Is my late father.

5
My wife
Is my father's verbal prayers
For my happiness.

6
I'm not abandoned.
The scent of my village
Lives in my heart.

7
An inscription:
Not caring for the World Bank,
My soul is my guide.

8
In the stream,
There is a black-and-white film,
And a future palette.

9
My mojo working:
Has my land
Recovered?

10
Before my eyes,
My village trees glow
In my exile.

11
Is it past greeting
Or future forgiveness?
My moon says, 'Hi."

12
Haiku company:
I have never forgotten
My pulse or village.

13
A fertile land:
The helpless create this narrowness.
My heart is wide.

14
Haiku hunters
Use nature as a bait
In extinct seasons.

15
Turning point:
I'll restore my land
In human haikus.

16
Helpless,
Enjoy your "nature"
And death.

17
The meeting point
Of light and darkness play
My Nile symphony.

April 2, 2019

Without Google Maps

1
A frog sound in stream:
As if I were in my birthplace
Erasing time's impacts.

2
Clock strokes:
I'm stuck in my memories.
How can time pass?

3
Off-memory:
My car's compass shows all directions
To my boiling heart.

4
A dormant volcano:
My memory denies my photo album,
So I invent my past.

5
A memory card
Accommodates unlimited data
With no trace of me.

6
Farm sounds:
The scent of this foreign farm
Is a time machine.

7
Good news.
This scent saves my memory
From its drought years.

8
Drought years:
This pharaoh does not grow wheat
Or have dream signals.

9
A red traffic light:
All cars are driving
Towards apocalypse.

10
An earthquake:
The ground swallows everything,
Even temples and screens.

11
Transmission outage:
The hands sprouting from the soil
Are transmission stations.

12
GPS:
I follow nascent farm scents
Without Google maps.

August 5, 2017

An Ascendance Bridge

1
Without a bridge,
I have to cross the abyss
In my foggy land.

2
Abyssal dense fog:
Are my eyes cloudy,
Or is the road a trap?

3
Associations:
Migration road is easy to take.
How to circumvent it?

4
An impossible road:
Come back, fighter of the fog;
Your land is memory.

5
I'm stubborn.
I mix times with winds of places
And laugh at my insight mills.

6
This mill is real.
I won't ask how to grind it
Or why it grinds me!

7
Fuss:
My hand is not white
In this fog.

8
Back to whiteness:
I'll part too.
History is a circle.

9
Orbits:
I'll cross these foggy layers
And return to myself.

10
Welcome back:
This helpless fuss doesn't know
How to ascend.

11
Arrival station:
I see me drinking myself
In this now-full cup.

12
Fresh cool pure water:
My dissociation is a bridge
Of action and arrival.

July 17, 2017

Speedy Recovery

1
Echo of the voice
Flowing the universe
Is in my heart.

2
My stubborn land,
I chant your name, and you call
For my death.

3
My land,
Do you have a soul
Away from me?

4
Your voice
Is clear in my dream,
Lulling me to light.

5
Unlike my dreams,
When I get up, you greet me
With indifference.

6
River fork:
Cheers, our future reunion!
Now, separate ways

7
I'll assume
I'm your father,
My motherland.

8
Your kids' clear voices
Are a gravity that makes us
Orbit around you.

9
My resources
Allow me now to adopt you,
My mother.

10
In my exile,
I hear this flowing voice
At your place.

11
My lady,
Who will return the greeting
At a distance?

July 10, 2017

A Unique Road

1
Mango and dates juice:
I'm here and there
Having many roots.

2
A old-time sip,
A sip in the future:
I'm the barzakh.

3
Welcome my friends.
We're meeting from times and places
On this mountain.

4
My tongue
Dives into my memory
And catches roots.

5
My people
Deny their memory
And adopt others'?

6
Let's eat
My fresh alphabet.
Welcome, Judas.

7
Do you
Deny my language and me now?
I'm a root.

8
This Facebook
Is a summer's cloud
In drought times.

9
This cup
Is a palm tree in a mango.
I climb both.

10
My resilience
Is fresh breath and this sip
Is a universe.

11
Why do I see
Trains of marching soldiers, friends?
Back to our cocoons.

12
Spiritual songs:
Our cocoons
Glow with us.

13
Threshold Fighting:
I see these soldiers naked
In a wilderness.

14
A private trail:
The mango tree fruits
In my head and heart.

15
My winning shadow
Shows me as mirrors
And visions.

16
I want to stop:
Mountain high pressure
Worries about me.

17
This cup
Is a ship and ocean
On the mountain.

18
My resilience
Is a unique road summoning
My ark and me.

19
I'll sail now,
Pitying those who are mad
At water.

20
This mountain
Illuminates my ark
With myriad fruits.

21
Fresh air:
I swim in the basin of light
Amid the garden.

July 9, 2017

Transformations

1
A bewildered bird:
Has he come home
Like me?

2
Where is my tree?
My inscribed name is a trapped
Bird song.

3
Within my view,
Lost birds and trees
Fathom my memory.

4
A landing bird
Picks my head
In my memory.

5
Silent emptiness:
I dive into the fullness
Of my memory.

6
This bird
Picks the handle of my bag,
Looking at me.

7
On travel road,
My bird and I are audience.
Of flying old wings.

8
Outside my car,
Memory birds meet there
On a tree.

July 14, 2017

Taxes

1
A cross:
High taxes
here and at home.

2
There,
Roots and guillotines
Exchange roles.

3
Here,
A livelihood and guillotines.
What is home?

4
Colonized there,
Dwarfed here.
A place or places?

5
A passing relationship:
These truncated roads
Refresh me.

6
Roads to Rome:
"What does a road mean?"
The Nile asks.

7
A side road:
I'll do away with fuss
On my trail.

8
A secluded ear:
Voices are hands
That breach seclusion.

9
A distant seclusion:
My heart enjoys calmness
And distant voices.

10
Within the storm,
I make my future life
In my own image.

11
In this storm,
No greed, worry, or intruders.
Life is open.

12
Old ruins:
My eyes are ecstatic
And painful.

13
Rivers convergence:
I remember old scenes
With a smile.

14
A fair tax:
A memory occasionally flashes
In my head.

15
A new road:
Memories are recyclable
And rewarding.

16
In the horizon,
A future fruit winks at me
And smiles.

August 12, 2017

The Day I Rejoice Alive

1
Yesterday,
I drained my depression.
Why overflowing now?

2
Speak, vicious circle.
You are future minefields, &
What is my kids' life?

3
What am I to war?
Bombs are before and behind me.
Do I lust for power?

4
Broken compasses:
The mountain of light is dark,
And my soul is far.

5
An eclipse:
Where are neighborhood engineers?
This speech is grandiose.

6
A guillotine:
Now, I'm, the rogue, the engineer
Of our road!

7
A tumbled road sign:
On your screens, I plan crimes
And forge IDs!

8
A road-blocking wall:
Against my stumbling block
I'll bang my head.

9
An abyss:
My bursting blood doesn't open
Sleepwalkers' eyes.

10
Lord of empty words,
I will not surrender
In your minefields?

11
A bare road:
All directions are mirage.
My heart will guide me.

12
I will not worry.
I'll bring me back to myself
And embrace joy.

13
Peace be upon me
When I rejoice alive
In my land.

November 28, 2017/ May 3, 2019

My Island

1
This island
Is a universe full of me
And others' doubles.

2
That guy
Sees my island as his puppet
Parliament.

3
"I will exchange
This lost boy in the well
For a throne."

4
"We elected you.
The playground is in the spotlight.
Your crap is orders."

5
I elect on one.
These are a drunkard's hallucinations.
My blood is a map.

6
I don't imagine screens
Moving like snakes
In this playground.

7
Static screens:
Your sleight of hand is over.
I won't let you go.

8
Crossroads:
The view in a wild imagination
On these riverbanks.

9
Divergence point:
Torches here and there
Feeding on my heart.

June 11, 2017

Signs

1
A book Fair:
Honor constants
Are on the market.

2
My book:
My life is for sale
As a charity.

3
At an older feast,
Your likes stepped down
The ceremony.

4
Will we offer you
As sacrifice
In a future spring?

5
Eater of your kin,
What's your next move
To fill your cup?

6
Optical illusion:
You may see
My hand paralyzed!

7

A new capital city:
Your balloon is a fortress
In your nuts eyes.

8

A long fasting day:
This meal is too little.
Who is the breakfast?

9

Crossbones:
You burnt all dialogue channels &
Want to lead a life!

10

What memory?
Your hands wiped memories
And lives.

11

Shut up
And look at your black harvest.
I'm all vigilant now.

12

Voracious mouths:
Hands are digging a graveyard
For their harvests.

13
Forget my old face,
And my new one you won't see:
Where will you be?

June 24, 2017

No Peace

1
Hallelujah![9]
Halla la lujah![10]
Where is peace haiku?

2
This sniper targets
My imprint on this mosque:
How can I pray?

3
An Azaan & a Mass:
Crowds of worshippers on a bridge &
Blank eyes watching.

4
Fatigued years:
Has the masjid key
Been swapped?

5
"O bartender,
We invite you"[11]
To this farce.

---

[9] A Hebrew exclamation meaning "God be praised" or "Praise ye the Lord."

[10] The opening of a song be the Palestinian woman singer Reem Benna. It can be regarded as the Palestinian form of praising Allah in such a way, although the song itself neither proves nor denies this.

[11] "O Bartender" is an Andalusian Arabic poem by Abu Bakr ibn Zahr (d. 1119 AD).

6
Clear Sky:
He does not cry
When stumbling.

7
His voice
Settles in mercury fields
And cries.

8
My parts
Cry one another
In worship.

9
This is my DNA:
From a far distance,
I pray.

10
Seeds:
The bag of soil I keep
Is a land fetus.

11
In my heart,
This fire is bakery
And for other ends.

12
My pen
Is memory and land.
I'm not indifferent.

13
My grief
Brings Al-Aqsa masjid
To pray with me.

14
At a distance,
My heart performs ablution
With Al-Quds water.

13
Echoes of other hearts
Accompany my heart
To Al-Aqsa.

14
On a bridge,
Hearts gather, and officers
Ask for passports.

15
Wedding music
Floods my sorrow
And moves me.

16
In exile,
A bride plucks mint leaves,
And sings of home.

17
A black flower:
Without fig leaves, we are
Qabeel and Habeel [12].

July 23, 2017

---

[12] The Islamic versions of Cain and Abel.

Dead Harassers

1
On a road,
A dead leans on a dead,
Suspecting me!

2
A labyrinth:
I'll escape your smile,
And save myself.

3
On the main road,
Sleepwalkers move in on me.
I keep my eyes open.

4
Landslide:
Feet keep descending
And speak about life.

5
Verbal market:
Coffins strip every day
And harass itinerants.

6
Travelling
Keeps my ears and eyes
As filters.

7
Shut up:
My visions will floor you
In your sleepwalking.

8
On my road,
The dead ask me to follow them
As their disciple.

9
Scorching storms:
These roads antagonize me
And movement.

10
Stagnant water:
My heart revolts and raises me
On the mountain.

August 10, 2017

I Do Not Worship the Calf

1
When I look
At this speaker's shabby words,
I damn coups.

2
Open land:
A knot untied from my tongue
Without results.

3
A gate:
A coffin on the river surface
Running to a dam.

4
I run across streets,
Trying to know why the dead
Track me.

5
High dams:
My ears deny your big talk
An entry visa.

6
A river course:
I cross the foggy land
Amid my injuries.

7
Identical volcanoes:
We look for lost members
And count our deaths.

8
On the other shore,
There are no passersby or life.
This ad was a decoy.

9
Scarecrows:
Our cows' udders are plundered
In this tricky land.

10
A meeting point:
My road is an echo
Of mountaintop light.

11
Erased road sign:
Who has stolen your echoes
And left you meaningless?

12
I don't smell
My country's wind
Though I farm its land.

13
My land:
The river keeper hates milk
And vegetation.

14
Opaque faces
Cross this land of clear skies
During lasting drought.

15
A dead magnet:
Medicine becomes a deadly poison
And catches souls?

16
Alone, not lonely,
My heart accompanies me
In travelling the earth.

August 7-24, 2017

Memory Land

1
I fight
Big talkers and gravediggers
With my open eyes.

2
What brought me here?
What took me there?
This spaciousness is hell.

3
Shut up:
Now, my heart is a virgin voice
For my ears.

4
Those distant things
Polluted my heart's water here.
Bless indifference!

5
Without brightness,
How can my light
Flood this darkness?

6
A lonely desert tree:
Would I find my land a mirage
If I slept?
7

A ruined capital:
We believed the promises
Of simpering faces.

8
Not ruining anything,
Here I am, helpless
Among ruins!

9
An old film:
In my land's scenes, I am
A subversive background.

10
The World Bank:
Were our hands stuck,
Or were we nuts?

11
Vast destruction:
We are the liars and audience
Of these screens.

12
Let's
Reconstruct our memories,
Not stop or cry.

March 19, 2019

Genetic War

1
On life margins,
Despite the basins and rivers,
The living invoke drought.

2
Worshipping drought,
How can these people
See Allah?

3
Hating honey rivers,
Do these people's programs
Have viruses?

4
How can I
Enjoy honey rivers alone
In this abundance?

5
O, passersby,
What calls and turns you
Away from life here?

6
Fellow traveler,
Why do you so avert life
And dirty the river?

7
Separation Wall:
Between you and me
Are barriers you make!

8
My heart
Is rooted in the river
You dry.

9
Sweet and sour:
I cannot enjoy
Your barriers.

10
My heart
Sees the first garden
Here on earth.

11
Rainbows:
Don't stone my difference
With your misreading!

12
Premonitions:
Your self-inflicted tragedies
My heart has seen.

13
I have discovered
The starting point
Midway.

14
Water stream:
These boundaries move
With my heart.

15
You curse
Starting points and the road
And avoid destinations.

16
My denying friends,
Why do you stone the life
That gathers us?

17
You re-enact
A genetic war I haven't
Witnessed.

13
You
Fight life, yourselves, and me.
Let the future go.

May 7, 2018

Sufficiency

1
How can I
Follow you to that
Hell destination?

2
The river is love:
Don't ask me to glorify
Your drought.

3
Deny me!
I sing on the Mountain of Light
Of rivers and skies.

4
A hidden camera:
"Where are our fathers' lifestyles?
We are stuck."

5
I don't need a hook.
All these creatures
Are my friends.

6
Let light be my road.
This river passes
Through paradise.

7
Without a guide,
I trace my road after the light
And sing of meeting.

8
Slate one, take million:
Why doesn't this camera
Capture anything?

9
Clashes behind,
I'm now present in myself
Picking universe fruits.

May 16, 2018

Women Catcher

1
Dropping his hook,
A translator catches the aspirations
Of women poets.

2
Spilled milk:
Why does the anthologizer drop poems
By publishers' doors?

4
Juice of palm dates:
I'll forget a man's fingers groping
Words of women poets.

5
In this anthology,
I don't see the men poets I know.
What's the anthologizer?

6
Struggling country,
Why are your sons' selections
A midlife crisis?

7
A manuscript:
I'll turn my kindness
Against the intriguer.

8
Recycle Bin:
In the face of whims, my racism
Is a balance.

9
Anthologizer,
Why do you incite me?
I won't pass your masks.

10
Hollow moans:
Who falsifies history
In draft fonts?

11
End of text:
Publishers have open eyes
In the still pond.

April 7, 2018

On the Mountain of Light

1
A procession:
Who has seen or read whom?
The wind wails.

2
On this street,
There are bloody footprints.
Has the street turned?

3
A too long street:
Do my steps
Eat themselves?

4
I'm not hungry.
Why do my teeth chatter
As in a famine?!

5
A poem
Stumbles on me
As if I wrote it.

6
Is it me there?
I am clashing with fantasies,
Old and new.

7
A vicious circle:
I have made my magnetism
In a different field.

8
This poem
Cannot be true or false.
It wonders.

9
Let's play:
You pose a present question &
I a future one.

10
I can't hear you.
Your poem is too old
To move me.

11
At crossroads
I inhabit
Meta-time.

12
Come on, my times.
I'll stay for an hour,
And then go.

April 10, 2018

Palm Dates Mines

1
Am I dead,
Or is seclusion lively?
The world is a bird.

2
A bird surveys the sky,
Experiencing everything,
Not willing to land.

3
From the sky,
The bird views the nest
With sorrow.

4
This dance is standstill.
What does movement mean?
My heart is not here.

5
Dancers
Tread upon my body
And sing of my future.

6
Where is the light
At the end of the tunnel?
Where is the tunnel?

7
Is this darkness
The light of my gouged-out eyes,
Or am I awake?

8
War veterans:
I have faced seas of troubles.
These troubles are OK.

9
I see,
In this calm after the storm,
Future massacres.

10
Neither my hand
Nor my vote is intact:
Do I have a voice?

11
Leaders' smooth talk:
I have to build myself a palace
In this barren desert!

12
Who'll keep dancing?
Who'll bang their head against walls?
Who'll surrender?

13
I loved palm dates.
Until when will I escape
From a palm to another?

14
A palm trees line
Hands me to another:
Are dates mines?
15
Away from the storm,
I keep my candle,
And it keeps some light.

16
Away from screens
I keep my candle,
But it doesn't burn.

17
Are screens storms,
Or storms V.0 screens
In globalized terror?

18
Which is the origin?
Which is the image?
The storm or screen?

19
A dancing image
Draws me into belief
And makes me a witness!

20
My veteran eyes
See mines
In entertaining screens.

21
After clashing,
Those faces meet on street corners
As corpses.

22
Corpses of hostile parties
Hold hands in mass graves
And pose for group photos.

23
On my balcony,
I look at victory celebrations
Indifferently.

24
Both parties dance
As if the future of my kids
Were glorious.

25
Let's dance:
You bring a TV camera
And I bring knives!

26
On screens,
Our dance is lively,
As if we were clear.

March 29, 2018/ April 13, 2020

Sub-Headquarters

1
I'll await no one:
My imagination is a rocket,
And my dreams a map.

2
This spaciousness is narrow.
I'll close my eyes
And dive into my heart.

3
Off headquarters,
My heart branches in my mind,
And there I embrace life.

4
Shut up:
Let your hand be soil
And mine a hoe.

5
Their loudspeakers
Are bombs subverting themselves
In the audience's ears.

March 26, 2018

Voting

1
This present time
Worries my heart:
Are celebrations decoys?

2
This land
Suggests a fearful future:
Is time dead?

3
"There, faces are strange.
Here, familiar faces are gloomy,"
Says a caught immigrant.

4
Between a poem and another
Are souls crushed by their own land,
And hearts looking skyward.

5
I'm not depressed.
My hallucinations open space
For probable joys.

6
I ramble on
To survive the present abyss
And see tunnel light.

7
My friends,
Don't get depressed;
Life is a joke.

8
We won't jump
From this bridge;
The river will be real.

9
Let's celebrate our loss
And plan for another struggle:
The river renews itself.

March 3, 2018/ April 14, 2020

Relief

1
Clashing street voices:
An extended family
Is deadly silent.

2
Blood on streets:
A distant bird sings
Of the Garden.

3
My dad's photo
Resonates with wrinkles and grief
And asks me patience.

4
Early flood signs:
My heart worries about
My kids' future.

5
Without a bright future,
I turn my food on fire
And sigh my worries.

6
A too long road:
Will we reach our station,
Or will our souls falter?

7
A twittering bird:
Previous honey words led me
To these barrens.

8
My starvation
No longer believes
These honey tongues.

9
Dad,
Life here belies you;
Can you re-birth me?

10
Dad,
How to live without memories
Or a future?

11
A bridge:
This land uproots me:
Ahead with migration.

12
On the long road,
Souls fall on both sides:
My heart is in my mouth.

13
Dense fog:

Fires without end,
And a dead deluge.

14
A summer cloud:
Don't fail me, my strength;
There it is, the map.

March 3, 2018/ May 10, 2019

Morgue

1
A question pool:
Am I a random block,
Or has Ali Baba retired?

2
In time's barzakh,
I catch my slippery brightness
With my hook.

3
Abusive academic chores:
Are subsistence workers and I
Human beings?

4
I would say,
"This harvest is abundant,"
But where is home?

5
A bait and a catch:
These other homes are snipers,
But I'm a cat with lives.

6
My hand
Types "old world" instead of
"Current world."

7
Years overlap.
Have I lost my sense of time,
Or is the coming weighty?

8
No lessons or regret.
All these steps are misplaced.
Who stole the box?

9
Nothing outside the box:
Are they sly politicians,
Or do I deny my powers?

10
Lava:
I try hard
To keep my kids' life.

11
Volcano:
I try hard
To keep my pen alive.

12
Eruption:
The regime regards me
As a rogue citizen.

13
Am I nuts?
My hands are in snakes' nest,
Thinking they tickle me!

14
A red pen.
Is this red ink blood cells
Or censorship?

15
How come
Your hand is white?
My exile is a witness.

16
Hi, Plato.
Art is 3 removes from reality &
Screens are thirty.

17
My little head
Cannot accommodate
Such grand narratives.

18
Away is sanity;
Away is insanity;
Angels are confused.

19
In my solitude,
Intruders try to lure me
Back to the morgue.

March 2018

A broken counter

1
Sir,
Why do you eat your people
Instead of feeding them?

2
Looming death:
Is the counter of your days
Broken, sir?

3
Apocalypse:
My land
Longs for tomorrow.

4
How cam my land live
While its providers
Don't have new blood?

5
Amid hopes,
Our car runs out of ourselves
And needs new blood!

6
Are you nuts?
How can I push the gas pedal?
We are dead.

7
Run-out fuel
And a long road:
Is there an end?

8
On the road,
This nothing is a huge procession.
Will we die on road?

9
On the edge
Of this abyss
We fight for death!

10
On the horizon,
Trees and clouds are coming,
And this observer is blind.

12
After the elections,
Our voices are mournful,
And our hands bloody.

13
Red traffic light:
A market is full of goods &
Dead buyers and sellers.

14
A dead car
And a driver accelerating it:
Which is the dead?

15
All traffic lights on:
Am I the dead,
Or is it the street?

16
Before Bab Zuweila[13],
A driver with red eyes
Holds his car's tank.

17
"Rest in peace,
O the Messenger of World Bank,"
We prayed.

18
How can I
Re-dig the old well
Inhabited by serpents?

---

[13] In Arabic, it literally means the Gate of Zuweila. It is one of the remaining gates of old Cairo. When Hulaqu sent some messengers to Qutuz, asking the Egyptians to surrender to Mongol power, Qutuz killed the messengers and hung their heads on Bab Zuweila. In addition, when the Ottoman Empire conquered Egypt, it killed the last sultan of Egypt Tuman Bay II and hung his head on Bab Zuweila.

19
The serpents in the old well
Accuse me of being a serpent
That poisons them!

June 29, 2017

Time of Invaders

1
An awful salute:
On the horizon, a rude tunnel &
A disciplined march.

2
This noise
Is an old book:
Is it time travel?

3
Have I travelled
To the wrong time, or is it
Invaders' time?

4
In my hand's range
Are memory-free home photos
And a bag of memories.

5
This desert is polluted,
And so is the village in my blood:
Where is my city?

6
This mixer doesn't mix!
Who squeezed and drank me?
Who dismembered me?

7

My dad is in heavens,
And diabetic mom is bedridden:
How can my magnet attract both?

8

In the beginning
And in the end is an empty cushion:
Where is fullness?

9

I haven't shrouded him.
The soil has absorbed his blood.
Here are the flowers, red.

10

From my balcony,
I don't see passersby:
Is geography societies?

11

No one is in view:
Does the sea block
Memories and steps?

12

I'm fasting for long,
And my head is a swollen balloon:
Why don't I burst?

13
Long live… the unnamed!
No life is long,
And no hours are full.

14
I have no heart,
Or memories that can believe me:
Hell is an advance.

15
Wedges or obelisks?
My body's memory is drunk
And I can't see well.

16
Not being suicidal,
Is my endurance a frustration?
A tunnel without end?

17
My writing
Does not relieve my swollen head;
Am I a ghost?

18
Beside sleepers,
How can I hallucinate
Until I fall asleep?

19
Maps on hot tin:
Barbequed cats
And peoples suckers.

20
Buildings in the air:
Dead people on earth and sky &
A heart suspects the future.

21
Reshuffling papers:
Total obedience and traders
In downs and downs.

23
Scrawny alphabet:
Has its user blocked its food,
Or livelihood terrorized it?

24
That departing guy
Will be a memory soon &
We'll have him pure.

25
Groping in fog,
My hands catch opaque memories.
My memory squirms.

26
Where is the horizon?
I survey all directions
And see only a wall.

27
This inflation is balloons,
And the earth is all volcanoes:
Rejoice, shortsighted.

28
These bones aren't mine,
And my silent hands are a mask:
Survival for whom?

29
Mercurial currencies:
Rocks deride digging hands.
"Stone the smiling poster."

30
Without a guide,
My pressure will explode
And dethrone ghosts.

31
What about the end?
Hocus-pocus &
Eyes staring in awe.

32
Amid water and soil,
The seed has been lost.
Maybe it moved skyward.

33
I have many oars,
And my boat is old:
What is movement?

34
On the riverbank,
Withering trees
And sleepwalkers.

35
At the river bed,
Smoking boughs
And welfare councils.

36
On a black painting,
I see an old memory,
My signature removed.

37
My sure steps
Are a slippery vision
And a probable arrival.

38
Broken oars,
Sailors laughing at themselves
And boats heading upstream.

39
Ah
Ha ha
Restart

40
I sigh
When listening to a song
In unknown tongue.

41
Before a foreign song,
My head gets lost in dictionaries,
And my heart makes sense.

2017

Contrastive Haikus

1

V1
In my far silence,
Her voice shows up in my head
And we speak freely.

V2
Two silences,
And in-between are deaf conversations
And shouting voices.

2

V1
Without vehicles,
I wander among places and add
To a book I read.

V2
A city dweller
Looks at a stranger angrily
And closes his window.

February 16, 2018

Taking Risks

1
A broken compass:
How can I trace my trail
With a lost sea sign?

2
A dry sea:
Between jellyfish and transcendent petrol,
No road for return.

3
A jellyfish threatens me:
Have I come before petrol rise,
Or am I distingue?

4
Jellyfish invading the beach:
Lines of leaving vacationers &
Fishers with empty nets.

5
Why will I speak
While your ears are goalkeepers
Protecting your torn net?

6
Tell me
Something I can believe;
I'm words traveler.

7
I no longer believe
In either Sisyphus or Heracles,
And Isis deserted you.

8
This voice
Is full of camouflage colors,
And I don't believe or care.

9
This tree is full of
Thorns, serpents, fruits, pests & shades,
And I enjoy my naked eye.

10
Decayed wooden bridge:
Ignoring the guard's orders to cross,
I'll risk swimming.

11
Voices on flowery screens:
Egypt is far away from me,
But my resilience endures.

12
Tongues on different screens:
Victims and victimizers shape-shift,
And my resilience doesn't care.

June 30/ July 9, 2017

The Far End of Nothing

1
You are
In my mind and blood, & my heart
Is grieving for and by you.

2
Lightning and thunder:
An official giving a speech,
And a summer's cloud.

3
Underworld:
A citizen seeking shelter from bombing
And an official counting loots.

4
Fireballs in air:
An agency raising credit rating &
Terrified faces in wasteland.

5
Dropped black ribbon:
Knights at a gambling table
And dead crowds on streets.

6
Long road:
Despite my sustained patience,
My steps are eaten up.

7
On the edge,
I make a light at nothing's end
And close my insight.

June 30, 2017

Opening

1
Behind the sun:
This hell is promising.
Will things backfire?

2
A melting pot:
My soul purged &
My body precious again.

3
Welcome, my friends.
Let's hold our hands together.
We are meeting again.

4
A clear tunnel:
Allah has blessed our hands.
Here light is.

5
Blessed be Allah.
Here the sun is rotating.
Let's go with it.

6
A meeting road:
Our hands are a compass.
Let's work.

May 10, 2019

Printed in the United States
By Bookmasters